DISCARD

The Teen Guide to Adulting: Gaining Financial Independence

What You Need to Know About

RETIREMENT PLANS

JERI FREEDMAN

New York

Published in 2021 by The Rosen Publishing Group, Inc.
29 East 21st Street, New York, NY 10010

Copyright © 2021 by The Rosen Publishing Group, Inc.

First Edition

All rights reserved. No part of this book may be reproduced in any form without permission in writing from the publisher, except by a reviewer.

Library of Congress Cataloging-in-Publication Data

Names: Freedman, Jeri, author.
Title: What you need to know about retirement plans / Jeri Freedman.
Description: First edtion. | New York : Rosen Publishing, 2021. | Series: The teen guide to adulting : gaining financial independence | Includes bibliographical references and index. | Audience: Grades 7-12.
Identifiers: LCCN 2019013742 | ISBN 9781725340664 (library binding) | ISBN 9781725340657 (paperback)
Subjects: LCSH: Pensions—Juvenile literature. | Retirement income—Juvenile literature. | Finance, Personal—Juvenile literature.
Classification: LCC HD7091 .F84 2021 | DDC 332.024/014—dc23
LC record available at https://lccn.loc.gov/2019013742

Manufactured in China

CONTENTS

INTRODUCTION....................................4

CHAPTER ONE
START INVESTING FOR RETIREMENT NOW.........7

CHAPTER TWO
TYPES OF INVESTMENTS 21

CHAPTER THREE
GROWING YOUR MONEY........................33

CHAPTER FOUR
FACTORS THAT AFFECT INVESTMENTS 41

CHAPTER FIVE
PRINCIPLES OF SOUND INVESTING...............53

GLOSSARY 67
FOR MORE INFORMATION.......................69
FOR FURTHER READING........................72
BIBLIOGRAPHY..................................74
INDEX..77

INTRODUCTION

Students learn many things in school, including mathematics, history, English, science, and foreign languages. However, there are practical skills that one needs in the adult world that one generally doesn't learn in school. Finances are one major area that students will have to deal with as they prepare to take charge of their own lives. How people handle money when starting out will affect how much money they have in the future and their ability to do the things they want to later in life.

When people start their first job, they will most likely have the option of participating in a retirement plan. Making the most of retirement plans can ensure a secure and comfortable future. Many people don't understand how to use retirement plans and, therefore, don't participate in them. But failing to take advantage of a retirement plan may mean passing up the opportunity to earn money for the future.

When a person is young, it seems that retirement is a long way off. Many people put off retirement investing for too long. However, money invested when a person is young has a longer time to grow. The more years that money is invested, the greater the amount that is available when one retires. Further, when people start investing part of their income in a retirement plan from the time they first start working, they develop good financial habits. Because people are living longer than ever before, they are likely to live a long time after they

A human resources staff member discusses options for contributing to a retirement account with new employees.

retire. The earlier people start saving for retirement, the more secure and enjoyable their future will be.

The material included here provides readers with an understanding of retirement accounts and how to make the most of them. The various types of investments are discussed. Some retirement accounts are offered by employers; others are available to individuals through banks and investment firms. This guide describes a variety of investment types and explains how to analyze a stock. It discusses the factors that affect investments, including those outside individuals' control, such as changes in the economy. When investing in

INTRODUCTION

individual retirement accounts, a person is responsible for handling his or her own investments. Therefore, information is given about the different types of financial services firms and advisors that one can use to invest. This resource also provides general principles for sound investing that enable people to grow their investments and protect them. It concludes with some general advice for sound investing. Note that this resource is only intended to give the reader an introduction to investing. Before committing money, one may want to talk to an investment professional.

CHAPTER ONE

1 START INVESTING FOR RETIREMENT NOW

It may seem odd to start worrying about retirement when you are just starting out in life. However, the fact is that the earlier people start investing for retirement, the more money they will have when they need it. It's not just a matter of saving more. When money earned on investments is reinvested, the total amount invested grows faster. Each year the base of your investments increases to produce income. This practice is known as compounding.

In 1935, when the Social Security Act was implemented, sixty-five was chosen as the age for retirement because life expectancy was sixty years. Today, many people are living well into their eighties or beyond. A report by the US Department of Commerce states that, according to the National Center for Health Statistics, in 2010 there were 1.9 million people in the United states who were ninety years of age or older. The report projects that the number of people over age ninety in the United States will quadruple by 2050. According to a 2016 report from the US Centers for Disease Control and Prevention (CDC), in 2014 there were 72,197 people in the

United States one hundred years of age or older. That number is up 44 percent from 2000, and the death rate has been continuing to decrease. Thus, a young person today could live many decades in retirement. To do so comfortably will require a substantial amount of money.

THE CHANGING FACE OF RETIREMENT

The first type of retirement plan was the pension. In a pension plan, a company sets aside money to be paid to employees when they retire. The first pension plan was implemented in 1875 by American Express. The US Congress enacted the first income tax in 1913, and in 1914, the Internal Revenue Service (IRS) ruled that money paid through pensions was tax deductible. This action encouraged more companies to form pension plans.

In 1980, 46 percent of private sector employees were covered by a pension plan, according to Georgetown University Law Center. By the 1980s, advances in medications and better working conditions began to significantly increase life expectancy. Pension funds had to pay money to more workers for a longer time. Since the late 1980s, many companies have sought to reduce their pension expenses by shifting more of the burden of investing for retirement onto employees. The Revenue Act of 1978 established qualified deferred compensation plans in the section of the act numbered 401(k). These plans are commonly known as 401(k) plans. They allow employees to defer (put off until later) taxes on a portion of

People often remain active many years after retiring, so they must ensure they have the funds for the activities they enjoy.

START INVESTING FOR RETIREMENT NOW

their income by placing it in the plan. Some pension plans still exist in the twenty-first century, especially in unionized industries, such as auto manufacturing and teaching, and for government workers. Most modern pension plans are defined benefit plans. In such plans, employees' pension payments are based on how long they have worked for the company and their salary at the time they retire. However, pension plans have become increasingly rare.

Except for unionized employees, few people can depend on having a company-sponsored pension plan. They must do their own retirement planning.

According to the US Bureau of Labor Statistics (BLS), in 2018, only 13 percent of nonunion private sector workers had pension plans or combination pension and 401(k) plans, and 51 percent had only 401(k) plans at the companies where they worked. (In contrast, 68 percent of unionized employees had pension plans, as did 78 percent of public sector employees.)

RETIREMENT PLAN TERMINOLOGY

There are a few terms that one needs to know to understand retirement plans. An asset is any item of value. Assets include money, stocks, and bonds, as well as objects such as antiques, jewelry, and artwork. A stock is a small share of a company. A bond is a document that represents money lent to a company or the government by an investor. The company or government pays interest to the bond holder for the money that is lent. Banks also pay interest on money in a savings account. Principal is the actual amount of money a person has put into an investment. A dividend is a percentage of a company's earnings paid to stockholders.

An elective deferral plan, or deferred compensation plan, is any retirement plan in which a person can choose (or elect) to put earned money before paying income taxes on it. "Deferred" means "to put off until later." One pays income tax on the money when it is withdrawn from the retirement plan. A defined contribution plan is one to which both employees and the employer contribute money. A defined benefit plan is funded by the employer and distributed to a retired employee according to the salary and years of service. An annuity is an investment in which a person deposits a sum of money with a bank or investment company, and the company pays the person a set amount of money monthly or annually for life.

START INVESTING FOR RETIREMENT NOW

Thus, most people working at nonunion jobs are responsible for their own retirement.

TYPES OF RETIREMENT ACCOUNTS

There are several different types of retirement investment accounts. The most common are 401(k) plans and Investment Retirement Accounts (IRAs).

401(k) Plans

A 401(k) plan is set up by a company for its employees. Employees can contribute up to a specific percentage of their salary, for example 15 percent. Usually, the company will match, dollar for dollar, some amount of the money that the employee contributes, for example 3 percent. The company typically offers a variety of stock, bond, and money market mutual funds in which employees can invest. Money put into 401(k) plans is pretax dollars, which means that the amount people invest is subtracted from their income for tax purposes. They pay taxes on the money when they withdraw it. Under a 401(k) plan, employees can start withdrawing money once they reach age fifty-nine and a half. If they take money from a 401(k) account before they are fifty-nine and a half, they must pay a 10 percent penalty in addition to taxes. Employees are required to begin distributions at age seventy and a half.

SIMPLE 401(k) plans are similar to traditional 401(k) plans as far as employees are concerned, but they are designed

Forms are available to help employees calculate how much money to put in a 401(k) plan each month to reach their retirement income goal.

to allow small businesses (with fewer than 100 employees) to offer 401(k) plans by having fewer regulatory requirements.

If employees leave an employer where they have a 401(k), they can leave their money in the plan. Alternately, they can move the money to another employer's plan or place it in an Individual Retirement Account (IRA). This process is called a rollover. If they take the money out but don't put it in another retirement plan, they will have to pay taxes and penalty fees. People are allowed to borrow money from their 401(k) plans,

START INVESTING FOR RETIREMENT NOW

but they must repay it like any other loan. It is not a good idea for people to borrow from their 401(k) plans. The money that is taken out reduces the amount invested and having to make repayments means that the employee has less money to add to the investment, which defeats the purpose of having a retirement plan.

There are many advantages to having a 401(k) plan. First, the money people invest is deducted from their pay, so the process is automatic. This method encourages people to think of their available funds as the amount they receive in their paycheck, and to budget accordingly. Second, people earn money faster because the company usually matches a certain amount. The disadvantages are: the choice of investments is often limited to a few different options, and the investment company handling the plan for the employer often charges high fees, which reduces how much money participants make compared to other investment options.

IRAs

Only businesses can establish 401(k) plans, but individuals can open IRAs. Even people who have a 401(k) plan can have an IRA. In 2019, the amount a person can contribute to an IRA each year was $6,000 ($7,000 for people sixty-five or older). The amount people are allowed to contribute is adjusted annually.

There are two types of IRAs: traditional IRAs and Roth IRAs. In a traditional IRA, the money people contribute is subtracted from their earnings before they pay taxes. Thus, payment of taxes on that part of their income is put off, or deferred, until they take money out of their IRA. This type of IRA is best for people who expect to earn less money after they retire—such as those who plan to work less or not at all. Because their tax rate will be lower once they retire, they will pay fewer taxes on the money they take out than they would if they paid it at the time they earned it. People can only contribute to a traditional IRA until they reach seventy and a half.

President Bill Clinton signs the Taxpayer Relief Act of 1997. This legislation created the Roth IRA.

START INVESTING FOR RETIREMENT NOW

The second type of IRA is called a Roth IRA, after Senator William Roth, who introduced the congressional bill that created it. When people invest in a Roth IRA, they use money on which they have already paid taxes. However, any money they earn in the Roth IRA is nontaxable. That means they will not have to pay taxes on it when they withdraw it. Many people choose to stop working for their employer once they reach retirement age, but they embark on second careers. For example, they might start a small business or become consultants. Other people, including many who are self-employed or engaged in creative careers, also continue to work after retirement age. A Roth IRA is often the best for people who expect to have the same or greater earnings when they reach retirement age because (1) they can continue to contribute to it after age seventy and a half, and (2) the money they earn on their investments is not taxable when they withdraw it.

Some people choose to contribute to a 401(k) plan until they reach the matching limit or until they reach the maximum annual contribution amount. They then continue to save for retirement by investing in an IRA.

SEP Plans

A Simplified Employee Pension (SEP) plan provides small business owners with a simplified method to contribute toward both their own and their employees' retirement savings. In a SEP plan the employer makes contributions to an IRA or annuity for each person participating in the plan. This arrangement is called a SEP-IRA. A SEP-IRA account is a traditional IRA and has the same investment and distribution rules as traditional IRAs. SEP-IRAs are often set up by self-employed individuals or small family businesses because the amount that can be contributed to a SEP-IRA is greater than that allowed for a regular IRA. SEP-IRA contribution limits as of 2019 were the lesser of 25 percent of compensation or $56,000.

Owners of a small family business can set up a SEP-IRA, which allows them to save more for retirement than a traditional IRA.

START INVESTING FOR RETIREMENT NOW

Profit-Sharing and Stock Purchase Plans

Some companies have a deferred profit-sharing plan (DPSP). With this plan, employees receive a percentage of a company's quarterly or annual profits. There are usually restrictions as to when employees can withdraw these funds without paying a penalty. The company decides how much and how often to contribute to the plan, but it must have a set formula for how it divides up the profit.

A number of companies offer an employee stock purchases plan (ESPP). This plan allows employees to buy company stock at a discounted price. Some companies include this option in their 401(k) plan. If one works for a successful company, one may want to buy some of its stock. However, one should not put all or most of one's 401(k) money in any single stock, including that of the company one works for. If there is a problem that causes the company's stock price to go down greatly, one can lose a large portion of one's retirement money.

403(b) Plans

A 403(b) plan (also called a tax-sheltered annuity, or TSA plan) is a retirement plan offered by public schools and certain tax-exempt nonprofit organizations. Employees contribute pretax income to individual accounts. Employers can also make contributions to employees' accounts. People who choose to work for a nonprofit organization, such as a charity, that is set up as tax-exempt frequently have 403(b) plans. Employees of public school systems often have such plans as well.

457 Plans

457 plans are offered to government employees. As with a 401(k) plan, employees can contribute a portion of their pay before paying taxes on it. There are two types of 457 plans:

- 457(b) plan, which is commownly provided to state and local government employees
- 457(f) plan, which is usually offered to highly paid government employees

The major advantage of 457 plans is that they reduce the amount of employees' taxable income. Employees pay taxes on the invested money and any interest or dividends when they withdraw it. If an employee quits or retires before age fifty-nine and withdraws money from the plan, he or she does not pay a 10 percent penalty as is the case with 401(k) and 403(b) plans.

Federal Government Retirement Plans

Federal government employees are covered by the following two pension plans:

- The Federal Employees Retirement System (FERS), a defined benefit pension plan

- The Thrift Saving Plan (TSP), which is similar to 401(k) and 403(b) plans

A federal employee age sixty-two or older, who has twenty or more years of service, would receive a FERS benefit equal to 1.1 percent of his or her greatest three years of average earnings, multiplied by his or her years of service. Most federal employees contribute 0.85 percent of their pay to the plan, and the remaining amount is covered by the government.

Federal employees can contribute to the TSP just as they would to a 401(k). Federal employers contribute 1 percent of all workers' pay to the TSP, regardless of whether a specific employee participates. The federal government also matches dollar for dollar the first 3 percent of earnings contributed by an employee and $.50 per $1.00 for the next 2 percent of earnings.

Regardless of the plan available, many employees have not adequately saved for retirement. According to the Economic Policy Institute, in 2013, households that were between the ages of fifty-five and sixty-four had an income of $55,000 but only $100,000 saved in a retirement account. Many had nothing saved for retirement. People face many expenses in life, especially once they start a family. Therefore, it is best to get started investing for retirement when one is young and has fewer responsibilities, and to continue to do so throughout one's working life.

CHAPTER TWO

2 TYPES OF INVESTMENTS

Whether one invests individually in an IRA or through a company-sponsored 401(k) account, one will have a choice of different investments. The following sections will describe what each investment vehicle is, its pros and cons, and when and in what way it would be advantageous to invest in it.

MONEY MARKET ACCOUNTS

A money market account is much like a savings account, except that it usually pays a higher rate of interest. Money market accounts are offered by banks and investment firms. The major difference between traditional savings accounts and money market accounts is that banks lend money deposited in savings accounts to borrowers in the form of loans or mortgages. The banks pay savings account holders interest in return for using the money. Money market accounts work in a similar way, but rather than lending the money from deposits, the financial institution uses the money to buy and sell various currencies around the world. A money market account is often offered

TYPES OF INVESTMENTS

to investors who are investing money in a 401(k) plan or IRA. The account provides a place for investors to put money that has not yet been invested, and dividends and money from the sale of stocks, bonds, and mutual funds are placed into it.

MUTUAL FUNDS

A collection of investments is called a portfolio. Mutual funds are a way that one person can pool his or her money with other investors to purchase a portfolio of stocks, bonds, or other securities. Investors buy shares in the fund. The price of the mutual fund is called its net asset value (NAV). The NAV of a mutual fund equals the total value of the securities in the portfolio, divided by the number of the fund's shares. This price is calculated at the end of each business day and changes as the values of the securities held by the portfolio change. Investing in a mutual fund allows a person to invest in a variety of companies. In addition, these funds allow investors to buy shares of companies that are too expensive for them to purchase on their own. A mutual fund is managed by a professional, who chooses the stocks for the fund and decides when to buy more or sell them. This is beneficial for individual investors, who don't have to worry about these aspects of investing. There are mutual funds that specialize in all types of investments. Some specialize in stocks of companies in a particular industry, such as technology or health care. Others specialize in foreign stocks. There are mutual funds that specialize in large companies, medium-sized companies, and small companies. However, for a beginning investor, the best

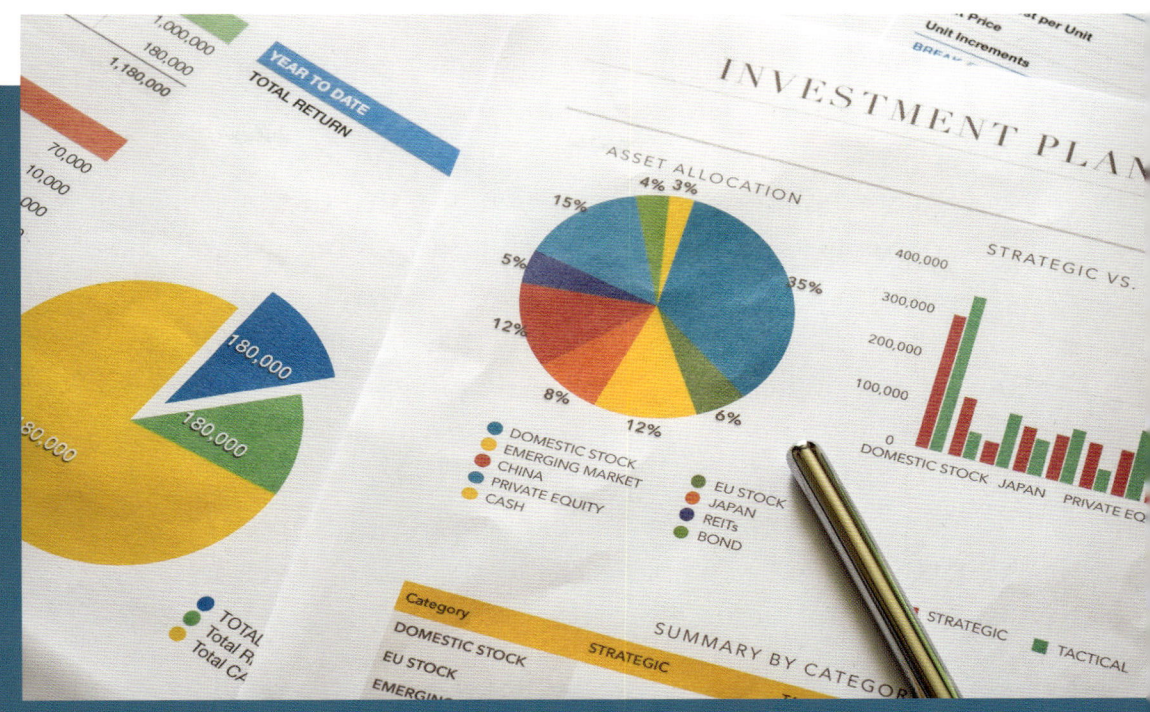

Investment firms, financial advisors, and company 401(k) plans provide investors with quarterly reports on the performance of the investments in their portfolio.

choice is frequently a diversified mutual fund. A diversified fund invests in the stock of companies in a variety of industries.

Mutual funds can be actively or passively managed. An actively managed fund has a manager who makes decisions about which stocks to buy and when to buy or sell them. A passively managed fund contains a set group of stocks that are the same as those in one of the major stock indexes, such as the Standard and Poor's (S&P) 500. The fees for actively managed funds are usually higher than those of passive funds.

TYPES OF INVESTMENTS

However, the managers of some active funds might be able to outperform a market index.

Mutual funds can be either load or no-load funds. Load is a percentage of the invested money that the mutual fund company keeps as a fee when a person buys shares. No-load funds do not charge a fee when a person buys shares. In general, it is preferable to purchase no-load funds when possible. When a person is considering purchasing a mutual fund, he or she should request or download the prospectus for the fund. A prospectus is a document provided by the mutual fund company that explains the investment strategy of the fund, the companies it invests in, its past performance, factors that could affect the fund, and the fees it charges. Investors should read the prospectus carefully.

EXCHANGE TRADED FUNDS

Exchange traded funds (ETFs) contain stocks in a variety of companies, much like a mutual fund. However, often ETFs hold shares of companies in a particular industry, such as biotech or energy. ETFs allow investors to choose investments by industry without having to choose a particular stock. Shares in exchange traded funds are bought and sold through regular stock exchanges. However, an ETF might not perform as well as the best company it contains because it includes poorer performing companies as well. Also, because ETFs do not provide diversification, shareholders can often suffer larger losses than with a diversified fund, if a particular industry is negatively affected

ETFs allow people to invest in a variety of firms within one industry—such as biotechnology—where the success of a single firm might be hard to predict.

by economic or political events. ETFs may be most useful for industries in which it is hard to tell which companies will be successful. An example is biotechnology, because it is hard to tell which company will be able to develop a successful medication.

STOCKS

A share of stock is basically a tiny share of a company. There are a number of different stock markets (also called stock exchanges). Two major ones are the New York Stock Exchange

TYPES OF INVESTMENTS

(NYSE) and the NASDAQ (the National Association of Securities Dealers Automated Quotation) system. Some 401(k) plans provide participants with the option of buying individual stocks, but some only provide a selection of mutual funds. IRAs allow individuals to buy both funds and individual stocks. To buy stocks, an investor places an order with a broker, either via phone or online. A broker is a person or company that carries out transactions between buyers and sellers. In addition to processing transactions, most brokerage companies provide a variety of online investment information and the option of speaking with an investment professional for advice and recommendations.

There are two types of stock: common stock and preferred stock. Common stock is the type most beginning investors buy. There are two major differences between common and preferred stock. First, the company decides whether common stock pays a dividend to stockholders and how much. The amount of the dividend might change over time, according to how well the company is performing. Preferred stock pays a guaranteed dividend, but the dividend never changes, even if the dividend increases for the company's common stock.

If a company goes out of business, the company's assets are used to pay off bond holders first, then preferred stockholders, and common stockholders last. Because the company may have no money left for common shareholders, they often lose their investment when a company fails.

There are two ways people make money in stocks. The first is an increase in a stock's value. When a company's revenues

A stock broker performs computer analysis on various aspects of a company and its stock before placing an order on a stock exchange.

TYPES OF INVESTMENTS

Some investors keep a close eye on stock price charts, which indicate whether the value of a stock is increasing or decreasing over time.

and profits are increasing, or when a company is developing exciting new products, people are often willing to pay more for it. Thus, the value of the stock increases. When a company's revenues or profits decrease, or the company has a serious problem, fewer people want to buy the stock, so its value goes down. The difference between what a person originally paid for a share of stock and its present value is called a capital gain (or capital loss, if its value goes down). Capital gains or losses occur, or are "realized," when the stock is sold. Some stocks also pay dividends quarterly or annually.

THE ROLE OF A HOME IN RETIREMENT PLANNING

Owning a home can play a significant role in retirement planning. The value of houses and the land that goes with them tend to increase over many years. This situation was true even after the economic crisis of 2008, when the value of many houses dropped significantly. Ten years later, many of the houses that had lost much of their value in 2008 were selling at prices equal to or higher than their price before the crash.

Owning a home captures much of the money one pays for housing. When a person pays rent, the money spent goes 100 percent to the landlord. When people buy a house, they usually do so with a loan from a bank. This loan is called a mortgage. The loan is paid back with a set amount each month. As the amount due on the loan goes down, a person acquires equity—the difference between what is owed and the value of the house. The equity is money that the owner gets back when he or she sells the house. When a house is paid off, the owner receives all the money the house sells for. In contrast, a person will get nothing back when he or she moves out of a rented property. On one hand, houses require repairs, which cost money. On the other, the monthly payment on a mortgage is frequently less than the monthly rent on a one- or two-bedroom apartment in the same area, especially when apartments are in high demand and supply is scarce. So, there is a trade-off. Houses also protect against inflation (loss of buying power of money due to an increase in prices) because they appreciate (increase in value) over time. A house acts as a piggybank. If one starts paying for a home in one's twenties or thirties, and keeps it or sells it and uses the money to buy another house, by the time one retires, one will often have an asset worth hundreds of thousands of dollars.

TYPES OF INVESTMENTS

BONDS

In simple terms, bonds are a loan to a company or government. When a company or the government needs to raise money, it often issues bonds. When investors buy a bond, they are paid interest at regular intervals, such as monthly, quarterly (four times a year), or annually. The amount of interest paid is called the bond's yield. People can buy bonds for inclusion in an IRA, or they can buy a bond mutual fund. Bond funds might be one option offered in a 401(k) plan. There are several different types of bonds, including the following:

- **Treasury bonds:** Treasury bonds are issued by the federal government for durations of two, five, and ten years.
- **Municipal bonds:** Municipal bonds are issued by city or state governments. The interest earned on many municipal bonds is not taxed if the bond holder lives in the state where the bond was issued.
- **Corporate bonds:** Corporate bonds are issued by companies. The interest rate on corporate bonds often varies with how financially sound the company is. Riskier companies often have to pay a higher interest rate than very sound companies to get people to buy their bonds.

Bond-rating companies such as Moody's Investors Service and Standard & Poor's evaluate each company's financial state and give its bonds a rating. For example, Standard & Poor's rates bonds from AAA to D, with AAA being the most sound. Bonds with very low ratings are sometimes called junk bonds. They pay a high rate of interest, but are risky because the company that issues them may go out of business.

Treasury bonds, also known as T-bonds, provide a secure way to earn interest on one's money.

TYPES OF INVESTMENTS

31

ANNUITIES

An annuity is an investment that pays a fixed sum of money to a person annually. People might purchase an annuity with money they have in their retirement accounts at the time they retire. A 403(b) plan might require a retiree to place a portion of his or her retirement money in an annuity. The amount the annuity pays depends on how much money the person invests. Annuities pay a set amount of interest on the invested money, such as 4 percent. The advantage of an annuity is that a person receives a set amount of money for life. The disadvantages are that the amount doesn't increase from year to year, so inflation eats into the value of the money received. Also, the fees paid to the company providing the annuity might be high compared to those for other investments. The amount of interest paid by the annuity might be lower than the return on other investments, such as stocks and mutual funds. To combat this problem, some firms offer annuities that increase when the stock market goes up, but that don't decrease in value when it goes down.

CHAPTER THREE

3 GROWING YOUR MONEY

The purpose of investing for retirement is not just to save money, but to make it grow. Investing in retirement plans enables people to accumulate a greater amount of money for retirement than by simply depositing money in a savings account. In addition, it protects the value of the money they put aside. Over time, prices for goods and services increase. This increase in the costs of goods is called inflation.

The result of inflation is to reduce the value of money. For example, $1 in 1900 bought about the same amount of goods as $29 in 2019. Inflation can have serious effects over a twenty-, thirty-, or forty-year period. It took almost $2 in 2019 to buy goods that would have cost $1 in 1990. Thus, if one starts saving for retirement in one's twenties by simply putting money in a savings account, that money will buy a lot less on retirement than at the time it was earned. Inflation is tracked by the Consumer Price Index (CPI), which is published monthly by the BLS. The CPI monitors changes in the prices of items in eight categories: food and beverages, housing, apparel, transportation, medical care, education, recreation,

GROWING YOUR MONEY

The US government tracks price increases in goods and services, such as groceries, to measure inflation.

and other goods and services. To avoid losing money because of inflation, one needs to put money in an investment that generates a return (additional money added to the invested amount) at least equal to inflation.

HOW STOCKS GROW IN VALUE

As mentioned, the two major types of investments are stocks and bonds. Bonds pay interest to bond holders. The interest paid on bonds is usually greater than that paid by banks on

COMPOUNDING

Compounding is the increase in the value of an investment; compounding interest is earned on both the principal and its accumulated interest. Compounding works as follows:

In year one, a person invests $1,000. The investor earns interest or dividends (a percentage of company earnings distributed to shareholders) on the investment equal to 4 percent annually. At the end of year one, the investment will be worth $1,040. If that amount is left in the account, at the end of year two it will be $1,081.60. At the end of ten years, the investor will have $1,480; at the end of twenty years, $2,191.

The formula for calculating the compounded return on an invested amount with monthly contributions to a retirement account is complicated. Luckily there are numerous compound interest calculators online that will do the math for you and allow you to test how much money you will make with different monthly contributions and rates of return. However, the following will provide you with a concept of how compounding with monthly investments works:

Assume that you invest $100 from your salary and that the average annual return on your investment account is 7 percent. An annual 7 percent return is approximately the same as a monthly return of 0.6 percent (six tenths of a percent each month). To turn the percentage value into a decimal number, you can divide the amount by 100. This equals 0.006.

You get the interest in month one by multiplying by 0.006 and adding this to the $100.

$100 \times 0.006 = 0.60$, $100 + 0.60 = 100.60$

The same result can be achieved simply by multiplying 100 by 1.006: $100 \times 1.006 = 100.60$

(continued on the next page)

GROWING YOUR MONEY

In month two, you add another $100 from your salary: 100.60 + 100 = 200.60, then you multiply the total by the monthly return of 0.006:

200.60 x 1.006 = $201.80

In month three: 201.80 + 100 = 301.80, 301.80 x 1.006 = 303.61, and so on each month.

Because of the effect of compounding, if you kept adding $100 per month and reinvested the amount earned, after one year, you would have $1,353.72. After ten years, you would have $17,610.41. After twenty years, the amount would be $52,800.41, and after thirty years, it would be $123,520.40. Thus, the sooner people start investing, the more money they make.

savings accounts. Therefore, in many cases it is possible to buy bonds that pay interest at a rate that is equal to or greater than inflation. Stocks grow in two ways: through dividends paid to investors and by an increase in the value of each share. The value of a share of stock can increase when many people want to buy it. It can also increase in value if a company buys its own stock from shareholders. When a company does this, the process is called a buyback. When a company retires the stock it buys, which means it is no longer available for sale, the result is fewer outstanding shares of the stock. Therefore, each share is worth more of the company's earnings.

Mutual funds are the most common investment vehicle in a 401(k) plan. The managers of mutual funds trade shares of the stocks in the funds throughout the year, resulting in profits. At the end of the year, the mutual fund gives, or distributes, those profits to the shareholders in the fund. The fund also distributes the dividends the fund has received from the stocks it holds. To maximize the amount one makes on an investment, it is important to increase the amount of money invested by reinvesting the money received in profits, dividends, and interest.

Large companies such as Berkshire Hathaway often buy back shares of their stock, increasing the value of each remaining share.

GROWING YOUR MONEY

GOING IT ALONE VERSUS USING A PROFESSIONAL ADVISOR

The first decision that investors face is whether to decide for themselves which funds or stocks/bonds to buy or consult a financial professional about what to invest in. The companies that manage 401(k) plans sometimes allow participants to consult with a financial advisor at the firm, either at will or during the quarterly periods when people are allowed to make changes to their portfolio. With an IRA, a person can choose to work with a full-service broker or handle his or her own investments. A full-service broker will meet with a client and provide a variety of services including retirement planning advice. Financial advisors often have a great deal of experience and are less likely to be influenced by the rumors and trends of the market than individual investors. Having someone experienced with whom to discuss investment choices can make an investor more confident about investing. However, some professional brokers push investors to buy stocks on which they receive a commission (a percentage of the purchase price paid to the broker by the fund company). Therefore, it might be best to choose a financial advisor who is fee-only. Fee-only means that the investor pays them directly and they do not receive commissions for selling stocks.

Discount brokers, such as Charles Schwab and E*Trade, process trades but do not provide extensive financial planning services or advice. At one time, discount brokerages

A financial advisor helps a client make a complete financial plan, including retirement planning.

only provided trading services to clients, allowing them to buy and sell stocks for a low fee but not providing any advice. Competition for clients has led some professional investment firms and discount brokers to offer their clients access to financial advisors whom clients can contact by phone for advice.

GROWING YOUR MONEY

10 GREAT QUESTIONS
TO ASK A FINANCIAL ADVISOR

1. What mix of investments would you recommend in a retirement account for someone my age?

2. What mix of mutual funds should I invest in?

3. Which stocks would you recommend for someone my age?

4. How risky is it for me to invest in Company X, Fund X, or ETF X?

5. What are the advantages and disadvantages of ETFs?

6. How often should I check on how my investments are doing?

7. Under what circumstances should I consider selling some of my stocks or funds?

8. How do the fees charged by the fund you are recommending compare to those of other, similar funds?

9. How much money should I keep in the money market account attached to my plan, given the current economic environment?

10. Are you a fiduciary? (Fiduciaries are advisors morally or legally committed to act in the best interest of their clients.)

CHAPTER FOUR

FACTORS THAT AFFECT INVESTMENTS

Many factors affect people's investments. Some factors are under one's control, such as how much to save for retirement. Others are beyond one's control, such as the state of the economy.

HOW MUCH MONEY DO YOU NEED IN RETIREMENT?

How much money people will need in retirement savings depends on the age at which they retire, other sources of income, the type of lifestyle that they expect to live, and where they choose to reside. The first step is figuring out how much one is likely to need annually. It's common for financial advisors to suggest a general rule such as 70 to 80 percent of one's salary. Other sources, such as the American Association of Retired Persons (AARP), recommend receiving 100 percent of one's salary for the first ten years of retirement. However, it is almost impossible to use a salary-based estimate when one is in one's twenties and just starting a career. For one thing, a person's salary will be much lower in their twenties than it will be as he or she approaches retirement age. For another, a person approaching retirement age might have a much larger salary than he or she needs for living expenses. That person might be spending only a portion of his or her salary and saving the rest. Thus, the salary doesn't really reflect the money actually required for living expenses.

Another factor is inflation. What might be sufficient for a person to live on today might be too little twenty or thirty years in the future. Therefore, people must periodically review their expenses and revise how much money they think they will need annually once they retire. If the amount one is currently investing for retirement will not provide that much annually for twenty to thirty years, then it is necessary to put more money aside. A number of websites offer online retirement calculators to help people plan how much money to put aside annually to achieve their retirement goal. These sites include investment firms such as Voya and Vanguard, and organizations such as AARP.

According to AARP, "for a retiree to generate $40,000 a year after stopping work, he or she will need savings of about $1.18 million to support a 30-year retirement; this was calculated using average returns of 6 percent and inflation at 2.5 percent, according to Morningstar, a Chicago-based investment-research firm." There are some factors that affect this number, however. The first is that it is based on living on the dividends and interest from the money one has invested and not taking any of the principal from one's investment account.

People who start contributing to a retirement plan while they're young might be able to retire at an earlier age and immediately pursue other hobbies such as traveling.

FACTORS THAT AFFECT INVESTMENTS

Using online retirement calculators, a person can review his or her financial situation and experiment with different investment amounts, timeframes, and retirement ages.

However, in the 2000s, dividend payments and bond yields are very low and might not produce sufficient income. Stock prices, in contrast, have risen significantly. Therefore, many financial advisors have stopped recommending living on income from investments and instead support taking out a total of 4 percent of one's combined income and principal annually. This approach is called the 4 percent rule. For example, if a person has $1 million saved for retirement, he or she could take out $40,000 each year. This amount assumes an average 7 percent annual return and 3 percent inflation, according to Michelle Brownstein, director of private client services at Personal Capital in San Francisco. (Some years the stock market generates a higher return and some years a lower return or a loss, but the amount of return averages out to 10 percent over time.) It is important to note that the 4 percent includes both dividends and principal removed.

A second factor that affects how much one needs in retirement is other sources of income. If one has Social Security or pension income, if one has nonretirement account investments, or if one continues to work part time after retiring from one's main career, this situation will reduce the amount of

Many retirees start home-based businesses after they retire in order to earn some additional income. Online marketplaces like Etsy and eBay have made this transition easier.

FACTORS THAT AFFECT INVESTMENTS

retirement account funds that are needed monthly. Often people buy a large house when they have children. After retiring, people often sell the house. If one sells a house and moves to smaller living accommodations, these actions can yield a large sum of money to be used for living expenses.

Third, where one lives affects how much money one will need. GOBankingRates.com carried out a survey that ranked the states according to how expensive they were to live in. It found, for example, that Massachusetts was one of the most expensive states for retirees to live in because of the high cost of health care and utilities. Also, although federal taxes must be paid on tax-deferred retirement income when it is withdrawn

GAINING INVESTING KNOWLEDGE

Knowledge is the key to making good investments. Knowing something about the stocks and mutual funds you hold, as well as the economic issues that might affect them, will help you make better investing decisions. There are at least three major TV networks that provide information on financial and investment issues: CNBC, Fox Business News, and Bloomberg TV. There are a number of magazines and newspapers devoted to investment news. The *Wall Street Journal*, *Barron's*, *Investor's Business Daily*, and *Money* magazine have helpful articles on investing for retirement. General business magazines such as *Forbes* and *Fortune* can be helpful as well. All of these resources are available online. In addition, there is a wide range of investment books.

from a retirement account, not all states tax such income. Thirteen states do not tax retirement income, according to *U.S. News & World Report*.

HOW THE ECONOMY AFFECTS INVESTMENTS

Investments go up and down from month to month and year to year. Sometimes these changes are gradual. At other times they are sharp and cause great changes in the value of one's investment. Rapid swings in the value of stocks is called volatility. Even though the value of investments changes constantly, they still increase significantly over time.

The stock market is affected by the economic conditions of a country. If the economy is growing, then there is more demand for goods and services, and most companies have increased profits. This growth increases demand for companies' stock, and the value of stocks rises. If the growth in the economy slows, then the value of stocks falls because potential stock buyers expect companies to have lower profits, which makes their stock less desirable.

The fact is that the stock market has never lost money over any period of twenty years, including the Great Recession, which began in 2008, and the Great Depression, which began in 1929. Twenty years after the Great Depression, stocks were worth more than before it started, and ten years after the Great Recession stocks were worth more than when the market crashed. This fact supports the idea that it is beneficial to start investing sooner rather than later, because this strategy

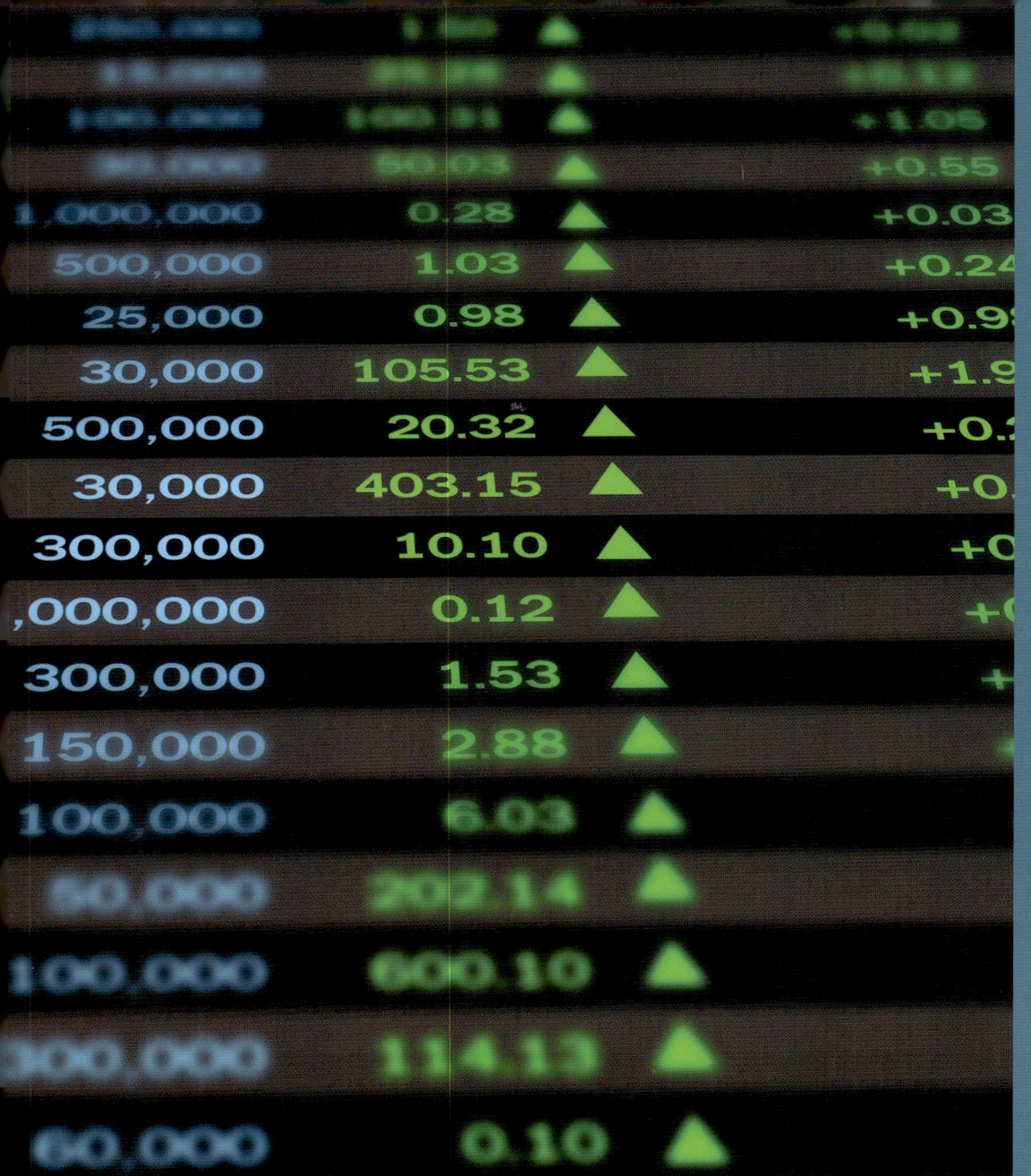

This display shows stock prices rising. When the prices for stocks continue to increase over time, this is called a "bull market."

WHAT YOU NEED TO KNOW ABOUT RETIREMENT PLANS

provides time to recover losses. It also demonstrates that even with great dips in value, stocks, and mutual funds that hold them, are good investments over the long term.

HOW ROBOFUNDS AND ETFS AFFECT INVESTMENTS

Recently-created types of investment funds include (1) those that invest automatically according to formulas programmed into computers, and (2) ETFs, which invest in the majority of companies in a given sector, rather than a specific stock. These investment funds often trade large quantities of stock in response to daily news on companies and the economy. This type of trading often causes violent short-term volatility in particular stocks; in all the stocks in a particular market sector, such as technology or health care; or even in the market overall. For example, some funds use computers that automatically make trades in response to key words in the news or in company earnings reports. Other funds automatically make investments according to formulas programmed into a computer. Such funds are sometimes referred to as robofunds. In such funds a computer might sell a large quantity of stock in response to a change in the chart of a stock's price, an announcement on TV about the economy or a company, or a headline in a paper such as the *Wall Street Journal*. These sales can cause the stock or an ETF that holds that stock to fall dramatically in price. Often another headline that is positive or provides further information will cause the same robofund and/or other funds to buy the stock—sometimes as soon as the next day. Similarly, because ETFs hold the stock of a variety of companies in one sector, a bad report, such as lower earnings by one company in the ETF, can cause investment funds to sell the

Robofunds use rules called computer algorithms to analyze data and automatically make trading decisions.

WHAT YOU NEED TO KNOW ABOUT RETIREMENT PLANS

entire ETF. Thus, companies in the same sector will go down, even though their earnings are great. In this way, ETFs and robofunds increase volatility in the market. However, because these changes in stock price do not necessarily reflect the real quality of the stocks, it is important for investors not to panic when volatility occurs. The best way to avoid worrying about short-term changes in the value of one's investments is to not check them constantly. Rather one should do so at regular intervals, such as quarterly or annually, and make changes that make sense at those times.

MYTHS & FACTS

MYTH **I don't need to worry about investing for retirement when I'm young. I have plenty of time to worry about that.**

Fact *Young people today will need a lot of money to retire in thirty years. One needs to start investing for retirement as soon as possible.*

MYTH **When the market drops, I should sell my stocks or funds because it might drop more.**

Fact *Unless there is a particular problem at a specific company, stocks that go down tend to go back up eventually. Since retirement money will be invested for a long time, it is better to just wait for the stocks or funds to recover or even buy more—and in some cases continue to collect dividends while you wait.*

MYTH **I should always listen to the advice of economists and other professionals I see on TV or read about in articles.**

Fact *Often experts disagree or have their own reasons for wanting people to buy or sell a particular stock. What you should gain from articles and TV programs is factual information on which to base your judgments. You can compare the performance of individual experts and identify the ones whose opinions seem to be reliable over time.*

CHAPTER FIVE
5 PRINCIPLES OF SOUND INVESTING

Choosing the right level of risk and the right mix of stocks, bonds, and mutual funds can produce a healthy portfolio that grows steadily over the years. The amount of risk and mix of funds may change over time, but the principles of investing will remain the same.

RISK AND REWARD

A central concept of investing is risk. When people invest, they hope that the value of their investment will increase. There is a risk, however, that the value of an investment could decrease. For example, a person could buy a share of stock for $10, and it could increase in value to $50 or decrease in value to 0. Some stocks are riskier than others. Frequently the riskier a stock is, the greater its potential gain. For example, if a person invests in a new technology company, that company might eventually become as large and powerful as Apple, Microsoft, or Amazon—or it might fail altogether. The advantage of buying such stocks when one is young is that, if the company

PRINCIPLES OF SOUND INVESTING

succeeds, by the time one retires that company might be quite large and the stock very valuable. Usually the stock of such new, or start-up, companies is relatively inexpensive. Therefore, the potential for gain is quite large in comparison to the amount of investment one will lose if the company fails. Young people have many years to make up for any such loss through gains in other investments.

Not all start-up companies succeed. Scott Eckert, the CEO of Rethink Robotics, was forced to shutter the company on October 3, 2018, due to its low sales performance.

WHAT YOU NEED TO KNOW ABOUT RETIREMENT PLANS

Different people are comfortable with different amounts of risk, and this situation will affect their choice of investments as well. Even if one doesn't want to invest in risky stocks such as start-up companies, young people will usually do better investing in stocks and stock funds than in bonds. Bonds provide steady income, but don't grow in value as stocks do. As one enters one's forties and fifties, it is appropriate to switch some of one's investments to bonds, which are generally less volatile than stocks. However, because people are living so long, most financial advisors suggest that even retired people keep some portion of their investments in stocks or stock funds because they will need to continue to grow their money in retirement for many years.

CHOOSING THE RIGHT MIX OF INVESTMENTS

One way to reduce volatility in investment accounts is diversification. Diversification means spreading one's money among different types of stocks and sectors. Stocks are divided into large-cap (greater than $5 billion), midcap ($1 billion to $5 billion), and small-cap stocks (under $1 billion). In general, the smaller the market cap of a stock, the riskier it is. Large-cap stocks often provide steady dividends, but the value of the stock does not usually increase as fast as that of small companies. Small companies often have a lot of growth. However, small companies usually do not pay dividends because they are reinvesting the money they make in order to grow. Having a mix of large and small company stock, or stock funds that specialize in these types of stocks, can provide a portfolio with both growth and income that can be reinvested.

Experts divide stocks into sectors--general categories based on industry. For instance, health care, technology, retail, and energy are all sectors. Most financial experts recommend that the basis of a retirement portfolio should be either:

- A diversified mutual fund, such as an index 500 fund (which includes all the stocks in the S&P 500), or
- Five to ten stocks or ETFs—in different industries

Sectors are important because when various events occur that affect the economy, companies in some sectors do well, and others do worse. For instance, when there is

WHAT YOU NEED TO KNOW ABOUT RETIREMENT PLANS

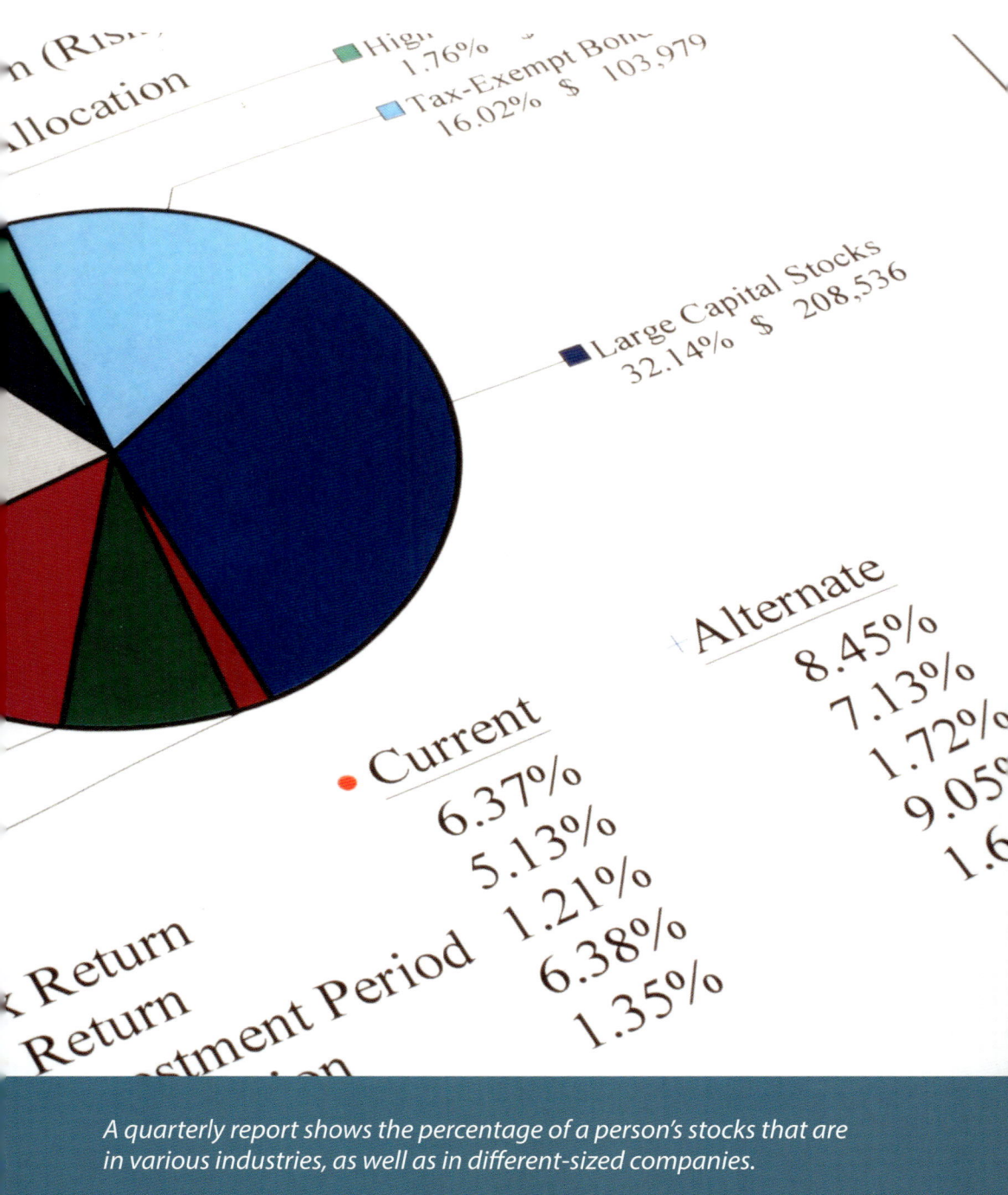

A quarterly report shows the percentage of a person's stocks that are in various industries, as well as in different-sized companies.

PRINCIPLES OF SOUND INVESTING

When the economy is good, people spend more money on items that are not necessities. These are called "consumer discretionary goods."

low unemployment and most people have money to spend, retail tends to do well. When the economy is doing poorly and people fear losing their jobs, they tend to cut back on spending. As a result, retail stores have lower earnings and their stock tends to go down. However, the stock of companies in the health care sector may do better than retail stocks because health care is a necessity, and in many cases it is paid for by insurance, not the consumer. If people have stocks in different sectors, then their losses are likely to be lower because as stocks in one sector decline, those in another may rise, reducing losses.

HOW TO COMPARE MUTUAL FUNDS

In most cases, 401(k) plans provide the option of investing in mutual funds. The issue is how to choose the funds in which to invest. The first consideration is that it is very difficult for managers—or computers—to outperform the standard

GETTING STARTED NOW

Students can learn about investing prior to enrolling in their first 401(k) or IRA. Using virtual tools allows them to learn what does and doesn't work before they invest real money. One way to learn about investing firsthand is by participating in an investment club. Many high schools and colleges have such clubs, which are supervised by a teacher. Students can invest either real or virtual (make-believe) money. In high school, if students use real money, then their parent or guardian must give signed permission, and an adult must place the actual orders to buy and sell the stock, because the students are minors. Whether they use real or virtual money, the students research companies, choose the companies to invest in, track their stocks' performance, and make any other investment decisions. There are also virtual investment simulators available online and through the Apple and Google Play stores, which can be used to practice investing.

indexes that measure market performance. One reason for this situation is that most mutual funds charge a management fee that is subtracted from participants' gains. Therefore, in many cases the simple solution is to invest a significant portion of one's money in an index fund that mirrors the S&P 500. At least this is a good choice for a first investment. S&P 500 Index

This overview of the S&P 500 Index fund includes information on the stocks in the fund, its past performance, and its fees.

WHAT YOU NEED TO KNOW ABOUT RETIREMENT PLANS

funds have very low fees because they do not require active management. The fund will go up and down with the market as a whole. However, when one analyzes the performance of the S&P 500 Index over its entire existence, it shows an average annual return of 10 percent. If one desires, one can add funds that have stocks not included in the S&P 500 Index, such as a foreign stock fund or a small-cap stock fund, for increased diversification. As one ages, one may want to move a portion of the invested money to a bond fund because, as a rule, bonds are less volatile than stocks. Also, toward the end of one's career, there may be a very large amount of money in one's retirement accounts. At that point, preserving it is as important as achieving additional gains.

All mutual funds have a document called a prospectus, which is available to potential investors. It provides a range of information on the fund's holdings, fees, and performance over time in comparison to the indexes that are used to track the performance of the stock market. The following are some points to take into account when comparing the funds offered in a specific 401(k) plan or being considered for inclusion in an IRA:

- The fund's rating from one to five stars, given by investment-rating company Morningstar. The rating tells you the fund's performance over a period of time. One can compare the ratings of the funds offered.
- The fund's performance compared to other funds that have similar holdings (such as large-cap

stocks, small-cap stocks, particular sector stocks, and so forth).
- The fund's top stock holdings; this detail is useful for buying funds with companies one would like to own, and to avoid buying multiple funds with similar holdings or buying individual stocks that are held by a fund one owns.
- The expense fees for each fund. The lower the fees, the more money the investor gets to keep.

It is important to remember that past performance is not a guarantee of how a fund will do in the future. Managers of funds change, and some perform better in some economic situations than in others. However, comparing these aspects will give one some guidance when comparing funds.

HOW TO ANALYZE A STOCK

IRAs and some 401(k) plans allow participants to buy individual stocks. There are a number of standard measures one can use to evaluate a stock. There are a variety of sources for information on stocks. Free online sources include Yahoo! Finance (yahoofinance.com) and the major brokerage companies that manage 401(k)s or IRAs, such as Vanguard Investments (vanguard.com) or Fidelity Investments (fidelity.com). There are also fee-based research resources such as Value Line (valueline.com). Although the format of the information varies, generally there is a search box where the user inputs the ticker symbol for the stock (one or more letters that identify a stock on a stock exchange). The information that appears looks similar to the following:

Excess Inc. (XS)

Last Trade..........................51.72
Net Change......................-0.75
Net Change %.................-1.45%
Bid......................................51.63
Ask......................................51.75
Day High..........................51.80
Day Low............................51.47
Volume..............................7,155,323
52 Week High..................55.93 on 12/23/2019
52 Week Low...................39.04 on 02/21/2019
P/E......................................11
EPS.....................................4.85
Dividend & %..................2.00 (1.60%)
Capitalization..................12.80B

"Last Trade" is the price that was most recently paid for shares of the stock. "Net Change" shows how much the stock has gone up or down in dollars and cents. "Net Change %" is how much the stock has gone up or down as a percentage of the previous day's selling price. "Bid" is the most recent amount offered for the stock. "Ask" is the most recent amount for which someone has offered to sell the stock. "Volume" indicates how many shares have been traded in the past day. "52 Week High" and "Low" are the

PRINCIPLES OF SOUND INVESTING

The New York Stock Exchange's display for Hershey shows information such as the company's lowest and highest prices for the day.

WHAT YOU NEED TO KNOW ABOUT RETIREMENT PLANS

highest and lowest price a share of the stock has traded for in the past year.

The next four items are those most commonly used to evaluate a stock. Investors use a measure called the "price-to-earnings (P/E) ratio" to see how much each share of a stock is worth. The P/E ratio is the price of one share of stock divided by the amount of earnings per share (EPS). For example, the price of a share of stock in Excess Inc. is $51.72, and its earnings per share are $4.85, so: 51.72 ÷ 4.85 = 10.66, which is rounded up to 11.

Thus, Excess's P/E ratio is 11. Generally, the lower the number, the better. For example, if two companies are equally promising, but one has a P/E of 10 and the other has a P/E of 15, the one that has a P/E of 10 is a better value (costs less per dollar of earnings).

A dividend is a percent of profits that the company pays to stockholders. Dividend in dollars and percent (Dividend & %) shows the current dividend that the company pays per each share of stock and the percent of earnings that the dividend represents. This measure gives one an idea of how much the company pays out to shareholders compared to other companies.

Market capitalization is the total number of outstanding shares times the price per share. Many company listings provide additional information, including financial information for

PRINCIPLES OF SOUND INVESTING

the past several years. From this information a person can tell whether the company is financially sound and if its revenues and earnings have been increasing over time. The stock of a company whose revenues and earnings are increasing faster than those of similar companies is likely to outperform the stock of those companies. The financial information also reveals how much debt (loans) the company has. Companies with less debt are less likely to run into trouble if a problem occurs. The report might also include information on the company's business activities, its position in comparison to its competitors, and prospects for the sector that the company is part of. All this information is important for making a judgment about whether or not the stock is a good investment.

Technical analysis refers to the use of accepted mathematical formulas and charts to evaluate stocks. Financial experts have developed mathematical measures that track various elements of stock performance based on theories developed by economists. According to these theories, certain patterns in the chart of a stock's performance indicate whether the value of stock is likely to increase or decrease. Referring to such charts can be useful for supplementing fundamental analysis. However, technical analysis alone is not sufficient.

Investing for retirement is an important part of being an adult. Starting young allows one to take advantage of compounding and save more money. It also enables one to invest in stocks with the most potential for growth. One should not be afraid of participating in retirement accounts. Investing for retirement can not only make one feel secure about the future but also provide the satisfaction of watching a nest egg grow.

GLOSSARY

annuity An investment in which a person deposits money with a financial institution and in return receives payments of an agreed-upon amount of money at regular intervals, usually for life.

ask The price that someone is offering to sell a stock at.

bid The price that someone is offering to buy a stock for.

broker A person who performs transactions between buyers and sellers.

capital gains Profit made when a stock is sold.

commission A percentage of the sale price of an item paid to the person who sells it.

compensation Pay, including both money and valuable nonmonetary benefits such as stock.

compounding The process by which interest is paid on both the original money invested and gains that have been reinvested.

deferred Put off until a future date.

degenerative Causing increasing damage to the body over time.

diversified Including many different types.

dividend A portion of a company's earning paid to stockholders.

earnings per share The total amount of company earnings divided by the number of shares that exist.

inflation An increase in the price of goods and services over time.

load A fee paid to invest money in a mutual fund.

market index A group of stocks used to measure the overall performance of a stock market. Examples of market indexes include the S&P 500 Index (500 large companies on the New York Stock Exchange) and the NASDAQ 100 Index (the largest 100 stocks on the NASDAQ stock exchange).

pension Money invested by a company that is paid to employees after they retire.

portfolio A collection of investments.

principal The sum of money a person puts into an investment.

prospectus A document issued for a mutual fund that provides information on its holdings, performance, fees, and other aspects.

sector A division of stocks based on industry, such as health care, transportation, or technology.

shareholder A person who owns stock in a company.

stock exchange A marketplace in which stocks are bought and sold.

tax-exempt Not having to pay corporate income taxes.

tax-exempt nonprofit organization An organization that is set up as tax-exempt according to the Internal Revenue Code (IRC) Section 501(c)(3).

volatility Sharp changes in the value of investments.

FOR MORE INFORMATION

Financial Industry Regulatory Authority (FINRA)
1735 K Street NW
Washington, DC, 20006
(301) 590-6500
Website: http://www.finra.org
Facebook: @FinancialIndustryRegulatoryAuthority
Twitter: @FINRA
FINRA is a nonprofit organization authorized by Congress to protect American investors, ensuring that the broker-dealer industry operates fairly.

Investment Industry Regulatory Organization of Canada
121 King Street West, Suite 1600
Toronto, ON M5H 3T9
Canada
(416) 364-6133
Website: http://www.iiroc.ca
Facebook: @iiroc
Twitter: @iirocInfo
This organization regulates stock transactions in Canada and provides information about stock rules.

National Association of Personal Financial Advisors (NAPFA)
8700 West Bryn Mawr Avenue, Suite 700N
Chicago, IL 60631

(847) 483-5400
Website: https://www.napfa.org
Facebook: @NAPFAFeeOnly
Twitter: @NAPFA
NAPFA connects people with personal financial advisors at all stages of life. Its members are paid by clients only and do not get commissions for the products they recommend.

New York Stock Exchange
11 Wall Street
New York, NY 10005
(212) 656-3000
Website: https://www.nyse.com
Facebook and Twitter: @NYSE
The New York Stock Exchange is the best-known stock exchange in the United States; its website provides a variety of information related to stocks.

US Department of the Treasury
1500 Pennsylvania Avenue SW
Washington, DC 20220
(202) 622-2000
Website: https://home.treasury.gov
Instagram: @TreasuryDept
Twitter: @USTreasury
The Department of the Treasury is the organization responsible for monitoring and managing the overall

state of the US economy. Its website includes the latest information on financial markets as well as information on the various types of bonds issued by the federal government.

US Securities and Exchange Commission (SEC)
100 F Street NE
Washington, DC 20549
(202) 942-8080
Website: https://www.sec.gov
Facebook: @SECInvestorEducation
Twitter: @SEC_News
The SEC is the organization that regulates investing in the United States. It provides educational written publications and a variety of useful calculators on its website.

FOR FURTHER READING

Booren, Steve. *Intelligent Investing: Your Guide to a Growing Retirement Income*. Greenwood Village, CO: Prosperion Financial Advisors, 2019.

Burkholder, Steve. *I Want More Pizza: Real World Money Skills for High School, College, and Beyond*. Encinitas, CA: Overcome Publishing, 2017.

Butler, Tamsen. *The Complete Guide to Personal Finance for Teenagers and College Students*. 2nd ed. Ocala, FL: Atlantic Publishing, 2016.

Friedberg, Jared. *Invest with the Best: A Teenage Guide to Smart Investing*. CreateSpace Independent Publishing Platform, 2019.

Gardner, Tom, and David Gardner. *The Motley Fool Investment Guide*. 3rd ed. New York, NY: Simon & Schuster, 2017.

Kobliner, Beth. *Get a Financial Life: Personal Finance in Your Twenties and Thirties*. New York, NY: Simon & Schuster, 2016.

Lyons, Darryl. *18 to 80: A Simple and Practical Guide to Money and Retirement for All Ages*. San Antonio, TX: Modern Growth Press, 2019.

McKenna, James, and Jeannine Glista and Matt Fontaine. *How to Turn $100 into $1,000,000: Earn! Save! Invest!* New York, NY: Workman Publishing, 2016.

Nydick, Harris, and Greg Makowski. *Common Financial Sense: Simple Strategies for Successful 401(k) & 403(b)*

Retirement Plan Investing. Melbourne: Lioncrest Publishing, 2018.

Slesnick, Twila, and John C. Suttle. *IRAs, 401(k)s & Other Retirement Plans: Strategies for Taking Your Money Out*. 13th ed. Berkeley, CA: Nolo, 2017.

Snow, Ted D. *Investing QuickStart Guide: The Simplified Beginner's Guide to Successfully Navigating the Stock Market, Growing Your Wealth & Creating a Secure Financial Future*. Albany, NY: ClydeBank Finance, 2018.

Tyson, Eric. *Investing in Your 20s and 30s For Dummies*. 2nd ed. Hoboken, NJ: John Wiley & Sons, 2018.

BIBLIOGRAPHY

Blank, Rebecca M. "90+ in the United States: 2006–2008." US Department of Commerce, November 2011. https://0.tqn.com/z/g/usgovinfo/library/nosearch/90_plus_in_us.pdf.

Brandon, Emily. "13 States without Pension or Social Security Taxes." *U.S. News & World Report*, April 1, 2019. https://money.usnews.com/money/retirement/boomers/slideshows/13-states-without-pension-or-social-security-taxes.

Brown, Jeff. "Is Spending Principal OK in Retirement?" *US News*, June 28, 2017, https://money.usnews.com/investing/articles/2017-06-28/is-spending-principal-ok-in-retirement.

Bureau of Labor Statistics. "51 Percent of Private Industry Workers Had Access to Only Defined Contribution Retirement Plans." *TED: The Economics Daily*, October 2, 2018. https://www.bls.gov/opub/ted/2018/51-percent-of-private-industry-workers-had-access-to-only-defined-contribution-retirement-plans-march-2018.htm.

Carlson, Robert C. *New Rules for Retirement: Strategies for a Secure Future*. Hoboken, NJ: John Wiley, 2016.

Connick, Wendy. "Are Target Date Funds Really a Good Investment?" The Motley Fool, April 12, 2017. https://www.fool.com/retirement/2017/04/12/are-target-date-funds-really-a-good-investment.aspx.

Fidelity. "What Are Mutual Funds?" Retrieved March 7, 2019. https://www.fidelity.com/learning-center/investment-products/mutual-funds/what-are-mutual-funds.

Georgetown University Law Center. *A Timeline of the Evolution of Retirement in the United States*. 2010. https://scholarship.law.georgetown.edu/cgi/viewcontent.cgi?article=1049&context=legal.

Internal Revenue Service. "Retirement Topics." Retrieved March 6, 2019. https://www.irs.gov/retirement-plans/plan-participant-employee/retirement-topics.

J. P. Morgan Asset Management. "Glossary of Investment Terms." Retrieved March 6, 2019. https://am.jpmorgan.com/us/en/asset-management/gim/adv/glossary-of-investment-terms.

Kane, Kayla. "How Long Will your $1 Million Retirement Savings Last? In Mass., Study Says 17 Years." *Sun Chronicle*, August 29, 2017. http://www.thesunchronicle.com/news/local_news/how-long-will-your-million-retirement-savings-last-in-mass/article_6447f2dd-61ca-5141-b47d-775a13bb5d6e.html.

Lisa, Andrew. "Alabama to Wyoming: The Cost of Living Across America." GoBankingRates.com. Retrieved April 25, 2019. https://www.gobankingrates.com/saving-money/home/cost-of-living-by-state.

Morrissey, Monique. "Private-Sector Pension Coverage Fell by Half over Two Decades." Economic Policy Institute, January 11, 2013. https://www.epi.org/blog/private-sector-pension-coverage-decline.

O'Hara, Carolyn. "How Much Money Do I Need to Retire?" *AARP The Magazine*. Retrieved March 11, 2019. https://www.aarp.org/work/retirement-planning/info-2015/nest-egg-retirement-amount.html.

Vernon, Steve. *Retirement Game-Changers: Strategies for a Healthy, Financially Secure, and Fulfilling Long Life*. Oxnard, CA: Rest-of-Life Communications, 2018.

Wall Street Survivor. "How to Compare Mutual Funds." Retrieved March 12, 2019. https://www.wallstreetsurvivor.com/starter-guides/comparing-mutual-funds.

Xu, Jiaquan. "Mortality Among Centenarians in the United States, 2000–2014." Centers for Disease Control and Prevention, January 2016. https://www.cdc.gov/nchs/data/databriefs/db233.pdf.

INDEX

A

actively managed funds, 23, 24
American Association of Retired Persons (AARP), 41–42
American Express, 8
annual adjustment, 14
annuity, 11, 16, 32
asset, explanation of, 11
automatic deduction, 14

B

Bloomberg TV, 46
bonds, explanation of, 11, 30–31, 34, 36–37

C

capital gains, 28
capital losses, 28
Charles Schwab, 38
CNBC, 46
common stock, 26
company/employer matching, 12, 18, 20
compounding, explanation of, 7, 35–36
Consumer Price Index (CPI), 33
corporate bonds, 30
cost of living, by region, 46

D

deferred profit-sharing plan (DPSP), 18
deferred taxes, 14–15
defined benefit plan, 11
defined contribution plan, 11
discount brokers, 38
diversification, 55–56, 58–59
diversified mutual fund, 23, 24
dividend, explanation of, 11

E

early withdrawal, 12, 18, 19
economy, changes in and effect on investments, 47
elective deferral plan, 11
employee stock purchases plan (ESPP), 18
E*Trade, 38
exchange traded funds (ETFs), 24–25, 49–51, 56

F

Federal Employees Retirement System (FERS), 19
fiduciaries, 40
financial professionals, reasons to hire, 38–39
457 plans, 19
Fox Business News, 46
4 percent rule, 44–45

401(k) plans, how they work, 8, 11, 12–14, 16, 18, 19, 20, 21, 26, 30
403(b) plans, 18–19, 20

G

government employees, 19
Great Depression, 47
Great Recession, 47

H

health care costs, 46
home value, and retirement planning, 29

I

income tax, 8, 11
Internal Revenue Service (IRS), 8
investment retirement accounts (IRAs), how they work, 13, 14–16, 17, 30

J

junk bonds, 31

L

large-cap stocks, 55
life expectancy, increase in, 8
load funds, 24

M

midcap stocks, 55
money market accounts, 21–22

Moodys Investors Service, 30
municipal bonds, 30
mutual funds, 22–24, 26, 30, 36–37, 59–62

N

National Association of Securities Dealers Automated Quotation (NASDAQ), 26
net asset value (NAV), 22
New York Stock Exchange (NYSE), 25
no-load funds, 24
nonretirement account investments, 45

P

part-time employment, 45
passively managed funds, 23
penalties, for early withdrawal, 12, 18, 19
pensions, history of, 8, 10–12
portfolio, 22
preferred stock, 26
pretax dollars, 12
principal, explanation of, 11
prospectus, 24

R

retirement, average age of, 7–8
retirement income, states without taxes on, 47
retirement plans, terms needed to understand, 11
retirement savings, how much

WHAT YOU NEED TO KNOW ABOUT RETIREMENT PLANS

someone should have, 41–42, 44–46
Revenue Act of 1978, 8
risk, as principle of investment, 53–55
robofunds, 49, 51
rollover, 13
Roth IRA, 14, 16

S

sectors, 56, 58
self-employment, 17
SEP-IRA, 17
simplified employee pension (SEP), 16
small-cap stocks, 55
Social Security Act, 7
Social Security income, 45
Standard and Poor's (S&P) 500, 23, 30, 31, 56
stock index, 23
stocks, explanation of, 11, 25–26, 28, 34, 36–37, 62–63, 65–66

T

tax-exempt organization, 18
Thrift Saving Plan (TSP), 20
traditional IRA, 14–15, 17
treasury bonds, 30
TV networks, as source of financial advice, 46

U

unionized industries, and pension plans, 10
utility costs, 46

ABOUT THE AUTHOR

Jeri Freedman has a BA degree from Harvard University. For fifteen years she worked for high-technology companies, where her duties included investor relations. She has been an active investor for thirty years. She has written numerous books for young adults, including titles on the economic crisis, women in the workplace, first bank accounts and investments smarts, and several career-related topics.

PHOTO CREDITS

Cover Kativ/E+/Getty Images; p. 5 Cecilie_Arcurs/E+/Getty Images; pp. 7, 21, 33, 41, 53 Zephyr_p/Shutterstock.com; p. 9 Photographee.eu/Shutterstock.com; pp. 10, 64–65 Bloomberg/Getty Images; p. 13 Casper1774 Studio/Shutterstock.com; p. 15 mark reinstein/Alamy Stock Photo; p. 17 Ariel Skelley/DigitalVision/Getty Images; p. 23 Montri Nipitvittaya/Shutterstock.com; p. 25 Dave G. Houser/Alamy Stock Photo; p. 27 Matej Kastelic/Shutterstock.com; p. 28 Vintage Tone/Shutterstock.com; p. 31 larry1235/Shutterstock.com; p. 34 Tyler Olson/Shutterstock.com; p. 37 Smith Collection/Gado/Archive Photos/Getty Images; p. 39 fizkes/Shutterstock.com; p. 43 sirtravelalot/Shutterstock.com; p. 44 Cheryl Savan/Shutterstock.com; p. 45 David Pereiras/Shutterstock.com; p. 48 iamharin/Shutterstock.com; p. 50 Tetra Images/Getty Images; p. 54 The Washington Post/Getty Images; pp. 56–57 Ryan R Fox/Shutterstock.com; p. 58 Anadolu Agency/Getty Images; p. 60 dennizn/Shutterstock.com.

Design and Layout: Jennifer Moy; Editors: Kathy Kuhtz Campbell and Wendy Wong; Photo Researcher: Sherri Jackson